Earth's
CONTINENTS

Continents

Bruce McClish

Heinemann Library
Chicago, Illinois

Customer Service 888-454-2279

Visit our website at www.heinemannlibrary.com

Designed by Stella Vassiliou
Maps and diagrams by Pat Kermode and Stella Vassiliou
Printed in China by Wing King Tong Co. Ltd.

07 06 05 04 03
10 9 8 7 6 5 4 3 2 1

Library of Congress Cataloging-in-Publication Data
McClish, Bruce.
  Earth's continents / Bruce McClish.
    v. cm. -- (Continents)
Summary: What is a continent? -- The make-up of continents --
Continental drift -- Plate tectonics -- Continental landscapes:
mountains -- Continental landscapes: erosion -- Oceans and continents --
Climate and continents -- Wildlife of continents -- People and
continents -- Relationships between the continents.
Includes bibliographical references and index.
  ISBN 1-4034-2986-3 (lib. bdg. hardcover) 1-4034-4244-4 (paperback)
  1. Continents--Juvenile literature. [1. Continents.] I. Title. II.
Continents (Chicago, Ill.)
  G133 .M355 2003
  910--dc21
                                    2002011594

Acknowledgments
The author and publishers are grateful to the following for permission to reproduce copyright material:
p. 5 Image Addict; pp. 7, 17 Auscape/Jean-Paul Ferrero; p. 8 © The Natural History Museum (London); p. 12 Auscape/S. Wilby & C. Ciantar; p. 13 Auscape/K. Schafer & Peter Arnold; pp. 14, 19 (bottom), 21 Coo-ee Picture Library; pp. 15, 16, 18, 19 (top), 24, 27 PhotoDisc; p. 25 ANT Photo Library/G. E. Schmida.

Cover photograph of the Purnululu (Bungle Bungle) Range, Australia, supplied by Coo-ee Picture Library.

Every effort has been made to contact copyright holders of any material reproduced in this book. Any omissions will be rectified in subsequent printings if notice is given to the publisher.

The author would like to thank: Avi Olshina, geologist; Peter Nunan, geography teacher; Craig Campbell, researcher; and Jenny McClish, researcher and contributing author.

Some words are shown in bold, **like this.** You can find out what they mean by looking in the glossary.

Contents

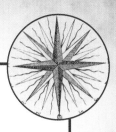

What Is a CONTINENT?

Continents are the largest bodies of land on Earth. Earth has seven major continents: Europe, Asia, Africa, North America, South America, Australia, and Antarctica. A continent is not the same thing as a country, though one continent—Australia—is also a country. A continent is usually much larger than a country. Its boundaries are determined by natural features such as seas and mountain ranges, whereas a country's border is decided by people.

Changing ideas

Ideas about the continents have changed over time. About 50 years ago, scientists believed the continents were fixed, standing in the same place for billions of years. Today, scientists know this idea is wrong. The continents are not standing still. Fossils give evidence that the continents moved great distances during ancient times. Measurements show they are still moving today.

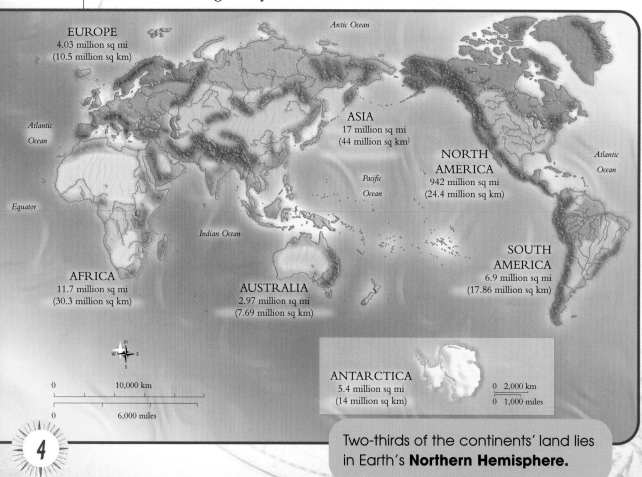

EUROPE
4.03 million sq mi
(10.5 million sq km)

Arctic Ocean

ASIA
17 million sq mi
(44 million sq km)

NORTH
AMERICA
942 million sq mi
(24.4 million sq km)

Atlantic
Ocean

Atlantic
Ocean

Pacific
Ocean

Equator

Indian Ocean

SOUTH
AMERICA
6.9 million sq mi
(17.86 million sq km)

AFRICA
11.7 million sq mi
(30.3 million sq km)

AUSTRALIA
2.97 million sq mi
(7.69 million sq km)

N
W   E
S

0   10,000 km

0   6,000 miles

ANTARCTICA
5.4 million sq mi
(14 million sq km)

0   2,000 km

0   1,000 miles

Two-thirds of the continents' land lies in Earth's **Northern Hemisphere.**

The lost continent

Atlantis is a legendary continent. It supposedly existed thousands of years ago, in the Atlantic Ocean. A Greek legend tells of an ancient civilization that lived on Atlantis, with great wealth, beautiful palaces, and powerful rulers. But an Earth-shaking disaster struck the continent and it sank into the ocean, destroying the people and their civilization. According to legend, the people of Atlantis had become corrupt and greedy, and their destruction was a form of punishment from the gods.

Joining the continents

The words used to describe the continents have also changed. For example, Europe and Asia are not actually separate bodies of land. Europe and Asia are joined in a more massive continent called Eurasia. Some **geographers** believe that Africa is not a true continent, either. It is also joined with Eurasia, and all the land together could be called Eurafrasia.

Although Eurasia or Eurafrasia may be more exact terms, most people still use the old names of Europe, Asia, and Africa when speaking of the continents. These names are familiar. People commonly use them when speaking about **culture,** travel, and world events.

Continents and Earth

The continents are more than great areas of land, or **landmasses.** They have an important effect on Earth, living things, and human history.

The movement of continents causes Earth-shaping events, such as the creation of mountains or the widening of valleys. The position of continents affects weather, the shape of oceans, and the pattern of their currents. The boundaries of continents often determine the natural range of different plants and animals—and even where different people live.

Continents contain a wide variety of landforms, including mountains and deserts.

The Makings of a
CONTINENT

Each continent is different in its size, shape, **climates,** and **cultures.** Yet all continents have certain things in common. They all have ancient rocks, including some that are billions of years old. They all have immense area of land. These range in height from below sea level—the level that is even with the surface of the oceans—to mountains that rise high into the sky. With so much land area, the continents contain a wide variety of surface features such as mountains, valleys, deserts, plains, rivers, and lakes. Some islands lying nearby can also be considered part of a continent. For example, Greenland, the large island to the northeast of Canada, is considered to be part of North America.

Continents and Earth's crust

All continents are part of Earth's **crust.** The crust is the outermost layer of rock that covers Earth. Below the crust are deeper, thicker layers called the **mantle** and the **core.** These deep layers of Earth are very hot and contain large amounts of **molten rock.** The crust has two parts: the continents, or continental crust, and the ocean floor, or oceanic crust. The continents are the thickest part of the crust, around 12 to 44 miles (20 to 70 kilometers) thick. The oceanic crust is the thinnest part. It is only about 5 miles (8 kilometers) thick. But the oceanic crust covers a much greater area.

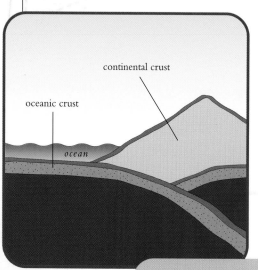

Rocks of the crust

Many different kinds of rocks are found in both the continental crust and the oceanic crust. Granite is a light-colored rock common in continental crust. A darker, heavier rock called basalt is the main kind of rock in the oceanic crust. Both granite and basalt are formed from different kinds of molten rock that have cooled and hardened.

Earth's crust has two parts: the continental crust and the oceanic crust.

Islands and continents

Australia and Antarctica are often called the island continents. However, although these continents are completely surrounded by water, they are not really islands. Real islands, such as Greenland and Great Britain, are smaller than continents. Australia, the world's smallest continent, is nearly four times the size of Greenland, the world's largest island.

Shields

Few areas of the ocean floor are more than 150 million years old. Several large areas of the continental crust are far more ancient, with rocks up to three and a half billion years old—the oldest rocks on Earth's surface. These ancient regions are called shields. A shield is the **exposed** core of a continent that shows ancient rocks such as granite. Shields can contain great wealth in minerals such as gold, silver, copper, and iron ore. The Canadian Shield covers a large part of North America.

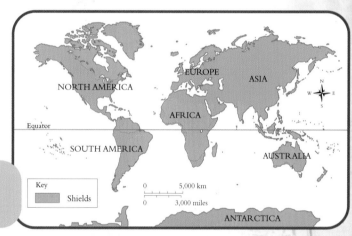

NORTH AMERICA

EUROPE

ASIA

AFRICA

Equator

SOUTH AMERICA

AUSTRALIA

Key

Shields

0   5,000 km

0   3,000 miles

ANTARCTICA

This map shows where the main continental shields are located.

Granite is a typical rock in continental crust.

CONTINENTAL DRIFT

Up until the mid–1900s, most **geologists** thought the continents had been in their current positions since Earth's beginning. After all, they argued, continents are part of Earth's **crust,** which is made entirely of rock. How could continents move, even slowly, when they are embedded in solid rock?

Lystrosaurus

The idea of fixed continents seemed to make sense. Even so, there were some problems. Among them was the *Lystrosaurus* puzzle. *Lystrosaurus* was a hippopotamus-like reptile that lived about 250 million years ago. Its fossil remains have been found on some of the different southern continents, such as Africa and Antarctica. But *Lystrosaurus* was a land animal. It could not swim. So how could this reptile move to such distant, unconnected continents, across an entire ocean? The same question had to be asked for several different kinds of prehistoric plants and animals.

Lystrosaurus and its relatives lived in prehistoric Africa, Antarctica, and India—which is today part of Asia.

Wegener's theory

In 1912, a German scientist named Alfred Wegener came up with a radical idea: that continents move along Earth's surface. This idea became known as the **theory** of continental drift. According to this theory, animals such as *Lystrosaurus*, moved throughout the southern continents because these **landmasses** were joined together 250 million years ago. This theory also explained why certain areas of different continents appear to fit together like the pieces of a jigsaw puzzle—especially the eastern coast of South America and the western coast of Africa.

Rejection

The theory of continental drift was not popular in Wegener's time. Continental drift may have explained why prehistoric plants and animals could spread so far, but there was little evidence that continents could actually move. Most geologists continued to believe that the continents stood still and they mocked the theory of continental drift. Any geologist who supported the theory was teased—or even dismissed.

New evidence

By the 1960s, scientific evidence began to support the idea of moving continents. Some of the most important evidence came from new discoveries about the ocean floor. These discoveries changed forever the idea that the continents—or any part of Earth's crust—do not move.

A daring scientist

Alfred Wegener was born in 1880. He became a scientist in the early 1900s. Although he mainly studied the weather, his most famous ideas were about Earth—especially his idea of continental drift. Only a few scientists accepted his bold idea at that time. Many other scientists would not listen to him because he was not a trained geologist. After Wegener died in 1930, his idea of continental drift became even more unpopular. Today, however, scientists recognize that Wegener's basic idea was correct.

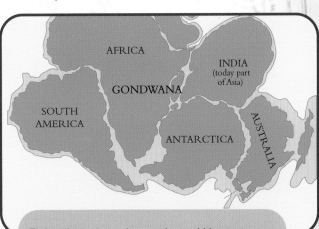

This diagram shows how Wegener thought the southern continents fit together hundreds of millions of years ago, before they drifted apart.

Plate TECTONICS

During the 1950s and 1960s, scientists made important new discoveries about Earth. They studied a long ridge beneath the Atlantic Ocean, where they found that the Earth's **crust** was splitting apart. As it split apart, the ocean was becoming wider. They studied the **magnetic properties** of rock around the area and found that the ocean had been widening for many millions of years. By the 1970s, most scientists no longer believed that the continents lay in fixed, unchanging positions.

Rigid plates

The new **theory** supported the idea of continental drift. It was slightly different from Wegener's original theory and explained more about how the continents move. According to the theory, Earth's outermost rocky layers are divided into huge sections of different widths and shapes. These sections are rigid, or unbreakable. They are known as plates, or **tectonic** plates. The plates are much bigger than the continents because they include parts of the ocean floor. This new theory became known as plate tectonics.

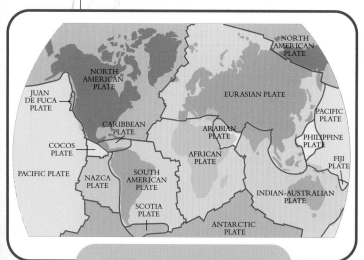

Earth's tectonic plates include both oceanic crust and continental crust.

Slowly moving

Tectonic plates are made of the rock in Earth's crust and upper **mantle**. Each plate is about 60 miles (100 kilometers) thick. The rigid plates float on the layer of rocks under them, moving sideways along the hot lower surface. When the plates move, anything attached to them moves as well, including continents and parts of the ocean floor. Scientists have measured how much the plates are moving. The movement is extremely slow—about 4 inches (10 centimeters) every year. But the plates can move great distances over millions of years.

Plate variations

Earth's plates have great variation in the area they cover. Most of them include both ocean floor and continental landforms. The Pacific Plate covers most of the Pacific Ocean floor, from western North America almost all the way to Asia. The Caribbean Plate seems tiny in comparison. It covers a much smaller area of ocean floor and a small part of Central America and South America.

Journey of the continents

Scientists believe that about 250 million years ago, the continents of the world all moved together into one giant supercontinent called Pangaea. By 200 million years ago, moving plates below Pangaea had split it into two smaller supercontinents. The northern one—called Laurasia—was made up of Europe, Asia, and North America. The southern supercontinent—called Gondwana—was made up of South America, Africa, Australia, Antarctica, and India. India was a separate **landmass** from Asia in ancient times.

Laurasia and Gondwana began breaking up about 150 million years ago. Europe and Asia remained close to each other. Africa and India drifted away from the other Gondwana continents and connected with the Asian landmass. South America drifted in a different direction, connecting with North America to form the Americas. Australia and Antarctica became island continents.

The continents that once belonged to Pangaea are now in very different places.

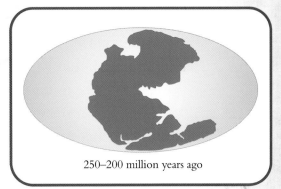

250–200 million years ago

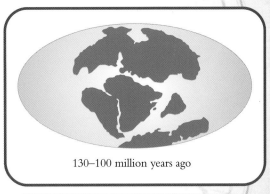

130–100 million years ago

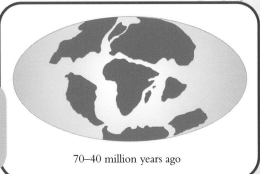

70–40 million years ago

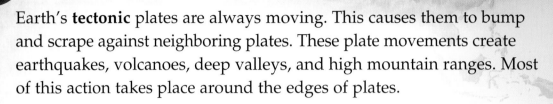

Earth's **tectonic** plates are always moving. This causes them to bump and scrape against neighboring plates. These plate movements create earthquakes, volcanoes, deep valleys, and high mountain ranges. Most of this action takes place around the edges of plates.

Moving apart

Sometimes the edges of two plates move away from each other. This causes a large crack, or rift, in Earth's surface. A rift is often accompanied by volcanoes and lava flows, as **molten rock** is pushed up from deep below Earth's **crust.** When two plate edges move apart under the ocean, it causes the ocean floor to spread out and widen. When two plate edges move apart on land, it creates a deep valley. If the valley widens enough, it may become flooded with lakes or seawater. The Great Rift Valley in eastern Africa is an example of two plate edges that are moving apart on land. Scientists believe the Great Rift Valley will continue to widen over millions of years, until it eventually splits Africa into two separate **landmasses.**

The Great Rift Valley in eastern Africa is located where two tectonic plates are moving apart.

Pushing together

As Earth's plates spread apart in some places, other plates must push together somewhere else. When the pressure of two plates pushing against each other is great enough, one plate drops below the other plate. This can result in violent earthquakes, lava eruptions, or changes to the crust. If a plate on the ocean floor pushes into the plate of a continent, it creates deep undersea trenches and chains of volcanoes near the coast.

Other times, when two continental plates push into each other, the land crumples and folds into a great mountain range. The high mountains of the Himalayas were created millions of years ago when the continent of Asia collided with the ancient landmass of India. Because of this collision, India now is part of the continent of Asia. Hundreds of millions of years before the Himalayas were formed, the Appalachian Mountains were created when North America collided with the Eurasian and African landmasses to form Pangaea.

Moving sideways

Sometimes two plates move sideways along each other's edges. This creates a break in the plates called a fault. The San Andreas Fault in California is between the Pacific Plate and the North American Plate. Plate edges do not move smoothly and steadily along faults. They move in sudden jolts—and each jolt causes an earthquake. Many devastating earthquakes take place along fault lines.

Some areas below Earth's crust are extremely hot, with huge columns of molten rock pushing upward. These are known as hot spots. When part of a plate moves over a hot spot, volcanoes can erupt through the plate. As the plate keeps moving, the eruption may continue, but in a different part of the plate. This is how hot spots form chains of volcanoes, such as the volcanic Hawaiian Islands.

Many devastating earthquakes take place along the San Andreas Fault in California.

Continental Landscapes:
MOUNTAINS

All continents have mountains and mountain ranges. Most of these mountains were caused by the collision of tectonic plates. Plate collisions may cause volcanic eruptions, or push or fold the rocky layers of continents into peaks and valleys. Mountain ranges are often near the edge of continents. The Andes Mountains follow the western coastline of South America and the Atlas Mountains are on the northeastern edge of Africa. They may also be in the place where two ancient **landmasses** were pushed together, such as the Himalayas, which join India with the rest of Asia, or the Ural Mountains, which join Europe with Asia.

The age of mountains

The shape and size of mountains often depend on their age. Some continents have high ranges with sharp, jagged peaks, such as the Alpine Mountains of Europe or the Rocky Mountains of North America. These ranges can be less than 60 million years old, which is young for mountains. Continents also have lower, more worn-down ranges, which can be hundreds of millions of years old. The Appalachian Mountains are the oldest mountains in North America. They were formed over 400 million years ago.

Older mountains, such as this range in Australia, are often low and rounded. They seem more like hills.

Mountains and weather

Mountains often shape the weather patterns on a continent. For example, a high mountain range near the coast can trap rain clouds blown in from the ocean. This causes much rain to fall on the coastal side of the ranges, but not much on the inland side. One side may have green slopes of farms and forests, while the other side may be dry, with only a few scattered plants. Mountains on the West Coast of North America create this type of **climate.**

Mountain facts

- Asia has the world's highest mountain range—the Himalayas.
- South America has the longest mountain range on land—the Andes Mountains.
- Antarctica has the coldest mountains. Many are buried by ice.
- Africa has many mountains, but few large mountain ranges.
- Australia is the flattest continent. It has the lowest mountains.

Dividing the rivers

A long mountain range creates a line of elevated land that forms an important boundary line for rivers. The elevated land forces rivers to flow in a certain direction. This kind of mountain range is called a continental divide. Rivers flowing down opposite sides of a continental divide move in opposite directions. In North America, the Continental Divide, also called the Great Divide, is formed by the Rocky Mountains. Rivers that flow down the eastern side of the divide head eastward toward the Atlantic Ocean. Rivers flowing down the western side head westward toward the Pacific Ocean.

Young mountains, such as the Grand Tetons in Wyoming, are often high and jagged.

Continental Landscapes:
EROSION

Many landforms of the continents, such as high mountains and wide valleys, appear to be permanent. But they will not last forever. They are always being worn away by wind, waves, streams, and ice. Even moist air or hot and cold temperatures can wear away land. The wearing away of the land is called erosion. Sometimes erosion takes place very quickly, but it usually takes place over long periods of time. Millions of years of erosion can wear down even the tallest mountains.

Shaped by erosion

Erosion shapes many features of the land. For example, as water and ice wear away a mountain, they slowly carve out peaks, **gorges,** and cliffs. As the mountain erodes, rock and soil are loosened and carried down the slopes little by little. Over time, erosion wears the mountain down to a smaller, more rounded shape. Narrow gorges become broad river valleys surrounded by low hills. Eventually, the mountain becomes a level plain. However, this kind of erosion can be interrupted whenever the action of tectonic plates causes the **crust** to rise up again into new mountains. Then the process of erosion starts all over again.

Rivers in high places often cut deep gorges into the land.

River erosion

Rivers normally begin in high places such as mountain slopes. They are created when rain or melting snow form tiny streams. These streams meet with other tiny streams and run together to form a larger river. The river keeps flowing until it reaches the lowest land, which is usually at the sea coast. As a river flows down steep mountain slopes, its current becomes very powerful. It moves quickly, dragging gravel and large rocks along the steep course. The rocks grind against the riverbed, deepening it into narrow, V-shaped gorges. When the river flows into lower and flatter areas, the riverbed becomes wider and the current becomes calmer. Instead of moving heavy rocks, the current carries mainly fine materials like sand and silt. Even so, the river continues to shape the land, creating wide valleys and **flood plains.**

Caves

Caves are often created by erosion. Water that seeps underground can dissolve certain rocks, such as limestone. The water slowly eats away at the limestone, making underground pockets, hollows, and tunnels. Over time, a great system of caves is created. Tunnels connecting the caves form many long passageways. Water flowing through the tunnels can form a river, or even underground lakes and waterfalls. The world's largest known cave system is in Kentucky. It contains over 340 miles (550 kilometers) of passageways, and scientists think it extends even farther.

When a river meets the ocean, it often creates a fan-shaped area called a **delta,** where tons of sand, mud, and silt are deposited.

Glaciers

Glaciers are masses of flowing ice. They usually begin in the high, cold slopes of mountains and flow down to lower regions. Glaciers move much more slowly than rivers. Like rivers, they pick up rocks and carry them along. The rocks grind and scrape against the landscape, carving huge U-shaped valleys into the land. They carve away mountainsides, wear down hills, and gouge deep hollows into the land. If a glacier reaches the ocean, it begins to melt and break into **icebergs.** Today, glaciers are found on all the continents except Australia.

Sheets of ice

A very large glacier is called a continental glacier. It is also sometimes called an icesheet or ice cap. Continental glaciers might cover a large portion of a continent or an entire continent. They occur in polar regions, such as Greenland and Antarctica. They have also occurred during very cold periods of Earth's history, such as an **ice age.** For example, vast areas of North America were shaped by continental glaciers during the last Ice Age.

Glaciers usually begin on the high, cold slopes of mountains.

Erosion in deserts

Hot deserts are dry regions mostly covered by bare rock and sand. Africa, Asia, and Australia have the world's largest hot deserts. These regions have little rainfall or ice to produce rivers or glaciers. But erosion still occurs in hot deserts. The land surface does not have soil or plants to protect it. When rain does fall, the water rushes across the bare ground, carrying tons of loose rock and sand into narrow channels called gullies. These are formed by the rushing water.

Waves pounding on the shores slowly wear away the land.

Carried by the wind

Desert erosion can also be caused by wind. Wind sweeping across the land picks up the dry sand and blows it away in clouds of dust. Heavier sand grains are blown closer to the ground, usually no more than a few feet (or a meter) above the surface. The sand grains are blown forcefully. They scrape and scratch against anything in their path. Sometimes they grind away the sides of desert rocks. Desert winds can also blow sand into large piles called dunes. Winds often change the shape and position of dunes. Shifting dunes in desert areas can cause problems by burying roads and even towns.

Waves

Wave erosion is caused by the combination of water and wind. Wind starts waves by blowing over the ocean. Waves move toward the land and break on the shore. The constant pounding of waves begins to erode the shore. Sea cliffs are worn down into rocks and rocks are worn down into sand. Much of this material is picked up by waves and hurled back against the shore, causing further erosion. Wave erosion shapes inlets, cliffs, rock arches, and hollows along the world's coasts.

Wind and sand can erode desert rocks, giving them an odd, mushroom shape.

Oceans and CONTINENTS

The oceans cover more than two-thirds of Earth's **crust.** The oceans are very different from the continents. Even the solid ocean floor is different. Rocks of the ocean floor are generally heavier than the rocks on the continents. Undersea plains are flatter than land plains and undersea trenches are deeper than land valleys. The Mariana Trench in the Pacific Ocean is the deepest known spot in the world's oceans. It is more than 6.5 miles (11 kilometers) below sea level—six times deeper than the Grand Canyon. Undersea peaks, cliffs, and ridges are often more jagged than those on land. This is because there is no wind or ice to cause erosion deep beneath the sea.

Widening and shrinking

Like the continents, the ocean floor forms part of the **tectonic** plates. This means the ocean floor is always moving, just as the continents are always moving. Undersea plates in the Atlantic Ocean move away from one another, causing the ocean floor to spread out and widen. In the Pacific Ocean, undersea plates move below the plates of the continents. This causes the ocean floor to become narrower.

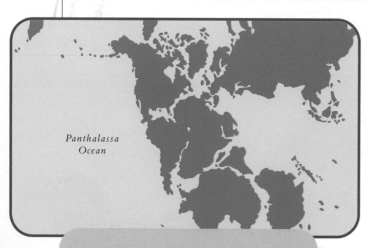

Panthalassa Ocean

250 million years ago, all the oceans of the world formed one great ocean called Panthalassa.

One ocean

The oceans have moved and changed over time. Scientists believe that about 250 million years ago there was one huge ocean on Earth, which they call Panthalassa. This was also the time when all the continents were pushed together into the supercontinent of Pangaea. When Pangaea began breaking up into different continents, Panthalassa began to break into different oceans.

Ancient floods

Sometimes the oceans flood over the continents, forming great inland seas where there once was land. This happened about 100 million years ago in many low-lying areas of Australia, during the **Age of Reptiles.** At other times, the ocean drops back from the continents, forming areas of land where there once was sea. This happened thousands of years ago during the last **Ice Age.** These changes can be caused by changes in Earth's **climate.** If Earth's climate is warm enough, the ice caps melt, causing the sea level to rise throughout the world and flood the continents. But if Earth's climate is cold enough, so much water may turn to ice that the sea level can drop to expose more areas of land.

The Mid-Atlantic Ridge

The longest mountain range in the world is below the Atlantic Ocean. The Mid-Atlantic Ridge is a winding chain of mountains that stretches for more than 8,900 miles (14,000 kilometers) in a north–south direction. The Mid-Atlantic Ridge has formed where two huge tectonic plates are moving apart, causing volcanic eruptions and the sea floor to spread.

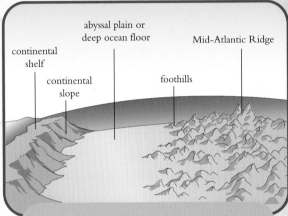

The continental shelf leads to the continental slope, which in turn leads down to the ocean floor.

The continental shelf

A continent does not normally end where its land meets the sea. Beyond the shore usually lies a part of the seabed called the continental shelf, which is covered by shallow water and is considered to be part of the continent. In some places, the continental shelf extends far beyond the coastline. A sloping surface called the continental slope forms the edge of the continental shelf and leads down to the deep ocean floor.

This ancient fossil lived in Wyoming when seas flooded the region during a warm period millions of years ago.

Climate and CONTINENTS

The **climate** of a place can determine what the land looks like, what kinds of plants and animals live there, the way people live, and whether there are many people or hardly any at all. Continents are so large that most of them have more than one kind of climate.

Sunshine

Most differences in climate are caused by varying amounts of heat and light received from the Sun. The tropics, a wide zone near the **equator,** receives the most sunshine. **Tropical** regions—most of South America and Africa—are mainly hot or warm throughout the year. This is a very different climate from the polar zones at the North and South Poles, which receive the least sunshine. Polar regions —Antarctica and Greenland—are always cold. Between the equator and the poles lie two large areas called **temperate** zones. In temperate zones, the amount of sunshine changes with the seasons. Temperate regions such as much of Europe and North America have hot, sunny summers and cold, gloomy winters.

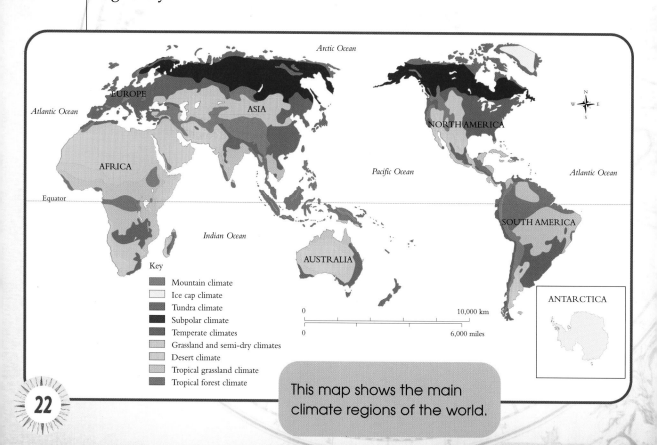

Arctic Ocean

EUROPE

ASIA

Atlantic Ocean

NORTH AMERICA

AFRICA

Pacific Ocean

Atlantic Ocean

Equator

SOUTH AMERICA

Indian Ocean

AUSTRALIA

Key
- Mountain climate
- Ice cap climate
- Tundra climate
- Subpolar climate
- Temperate climates
- Grassland and semi-dry climates
- Desert climate
- Tropical grassland climate
- Tropical forest climate

0   10,000 km

0   6,000 miles

ANTARCTICA

This map shows the main climate regions of the world.

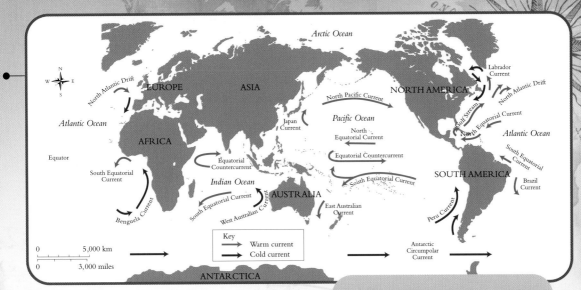

This map shows the world's oceans and their currents in relation to the continents.

Mountain climates

The climates of different regions on the continents do not always fit neatly into tropical, temperate, or polar zones. High areas, such as mountains, always have a colder climate than the land below because the air temperature drops as the **altitude** increases. Many tropical mountain areas of South America are high enough to have a temperate or polar climate—even though they lie in the tropical zone.

Wet and dry

Differences in rainfall can also cause differences in climate. Rainfall depends on many conditions, including the moisture in the air and the temperature of ocean currents. Polar regions are normally very dry throughout the year, but rainfall can vary a great deal in tropical and temperate regions. High rainfall can support thick, green forests, while lower rainfall can only support grass or small plants. If the rainfall is very low, the result is a desert climate.

Currents and climate

Ocean currents are streams of water that flow in a regular course through the sea. Some ocean currents carry warm water from the tropics into cooler regions, while others carry cold water from the polar regions into warmer regions. The temperature of currents can influence the climate on any land nearby. A warm current, like one along Europe's Atlantic coast, can bring mild winter weather to coastal areas, even when areas further inland are freezing. A cold current, like one along the west coast of South America, can bring cool summer fogs to coastal areas, even when areas further inland are hot. A cold current, such as the current that flows along the southwestern coast of Africa, brings mainly dry weather. A warm current, such as the current that flows along the east coast of Australia, brings much rainfall.

The Wildlife of
CONTINENTS

Each continent is known for its special varieties of plants and animals. For example, South America is famous for its rain forests and colorful birds; Asia for its bamboo forests and pandas; and Africa for its enormous grasslands with elephants, rhinoceroses, and giraffes.

Sharing wildlife

More than 200 million years ago, when the continents were closer together, most of them shared similar kinds of prehistoric plants and animals. Since then, the continents have separated, and this sharing has been less common. However, some continents still share many of the same kinds of plants and animals. North America, Europe, and Asia all have large forest regions of **conifers** and **deciduous** trees. Animals such as bears, wolves, lynxes, foxes, and deer live in these forests. North of these forests, in the cold arctic regions, there are animals such as polar bears, arctic foxes, reindeer, and seals. Europe and Asia share so much wildlife because they are close together, and this makes it easier for plants and animals to move between them. North America has much of the same wildlife because the continent was connected to Asia by a land bridge across the Bering Strait more than 10,000 years ago. The land bridge was formed when sea levels fell during the last **Ice Age.**

Horses first appeared in prehistoric North America. From there they crossed ancient land bridges, spreading out over Europe and Asia.

Ocean barriers

Some continents have plants and animals that do not live anywhere else in the world. For example, Australia is the only continent with kangaroos, platypuses, and emus—a type of large, flightless bird. This is because Australia is an island continent completely surrounded by sea. The sea acts as a barrier, stopping most animals—especially those that cannot swim or fly—from leaving or entering Australia.

Land and climate barriers

High mountains, hot deserts, and differences in **climate** can also act as wildlife barriers. Such barriers sometimes stand between plants and animals on the same continent. The Himalayas separate the wildlife of northern and central Asia from the wildlife of **tropical** southern Asia. In a similar way, the vast Sahara Desert is a barrier between the wildlife of northern Africa and the wildlife of southern Africa. Most plants and animals cannot endure the harsh conditions of these barriers, and cannot travel across them.

Wildlife facts

- Tropical regions of the world have the greatest varieties of plants and animals. Polar regions have the fewest.
- Africa has the largest land animals.
- South America has the greatest variety of birds.
- North America has the tallest and oldest trees.
- Australia has the most marsupials, or pouched mammals, such as kangaroos, and the only monotremes, or egg-laying mammals, such as the platypus.
- Europe and Asia have the greatest number of tame animals, including horses, cattle, sheep, goats, pigs, and reindeer.
- Antarctica has the fewest plants and animals living on land.

Lungfish are found in the southern continents of Australia, Africa, and South America. They are fish that can breathe using either gills or lungs.

People and CONTINENTS

The first people came from the continent of Africa. They crossed into Asia and Europe around one million years ago. The first known civilizations began in Asia, around 5,000 to 10,000 years ago. Early people used the gigantic Asian continent as a path to move into North America, South America, and Australia. They settled almost every part of these continents, including most of the nearby islands. They did not allow seas, mountains, or deserts to act as permanent barriers. Today, Antarctica is the only continent not permanently settled.

Populations

Human populations are not distributed equally around the continents. Most people live around a continent's rivers or lakes, or on its coasts or **fertile plains.** These are places where fishing, farming, trade, and transportation are easiest. People are far less numerous in mountain, desert, or polar areas.

Of all the continents, Asia has the most people. It has the world's most heavily populated countries—China and India. Africa and Europe also have large populations. Antarctica has the smallest population, with only temporary residents, such as scientists and tourists.

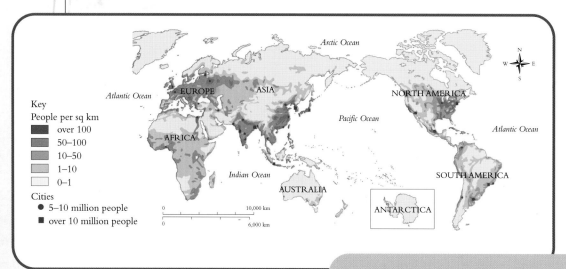

Key
People per sq km
over 100
50–100
10–50
1–10
0–1
Cities
● 5–10 million people
■ over 10 million people

This map shows where most people live on each continent.

Cultures

Plants and animals of neighboring continents share many similarities, while the plants and animals of distant continents can be very different. This sometimes is the case for people, too.

Immigration and settlement over the past few centuries have mixed up the places where different **cultural** groups live. In North America, for example, there are people from very different countries and many different cultures. Some people seem to have little in common. They may speak a different language. They may have a different religion, family customs, or diet. In a country like China, there has been much less immigration than in North America. People who live there often share the same religion, customs, and diet.

Resources

People living on continents take advantage of **natural resources.** These include plants, animals, soil, water, **timber,** and minerals. Continents such as North America and Europe are rich in most of these natural resources. But huge areas of Africa, Asia, and Australia have little water or fertile soil. Sometimes natural resources are used up quickly. Animals may become wiped out through too much hunting or forests may be wiped out through **deforestation.** People on most continents are taking steps to protect their natural resources, such as planting more trees, recycling, and using what they have more wisely.

European ways

Europe has had a major cultural influence on the other continents. From the 1500s to the 1800s, Europeans **colonized** most of the continents around the world, especially North America, South America, Africa, and Australia.

These continents now have **independent** countries with their own governments. However, many people on each of these continents still speak a European language or eat and dress in a European manner. European languages such as English, French, and Spanish are among the most widespread languages in the world.

Different continents have been at the center of human culture at different times in history.

Relationships Between
CONTINENTS

There are important relationships between the different continents, especially for those that lie close together. There are often similarities in the landforms, **climate,** wildlife, and peoples of neighboring continents. For people, similarities can result in lasting friendships, associations, and **treaties.** There can also be big differences between the people of neighboring continents, and these can result in disagreement, hostilities, and war.

The Old World

Geographers often group the continents according to their relationships. There are several ways this can be done. For example, Europe, Asia, and Africa are often grouped together. This makes sense, because the three continents are connected by land. But they have another relationship as well—some of the oldest events in recorded human history took place in Europe, Asia, and Africa. This is why these continents are sometimes called Old World continents. Some geographers also include Australia as one of the Old World continents.

The New World

North America and South America are also grouped together as "the Americas." They were settled in ancient times by Native Americans who came to live in almost every part of these two continents. European civilization came to the Americas more recently, along with modern cities and countries. For this reason, North America and South America are called New World continents.

This map shows some of the different ways the continents can be grouped.

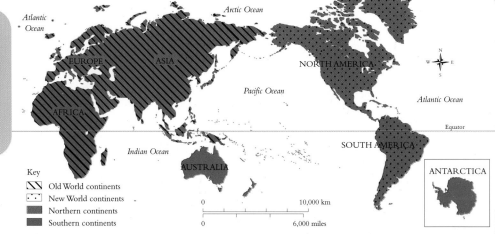

Island continents

Australia and Antarctica are completely surrounded by water and thus isolated from the other continents. These continents are often called island continents.

North and south

Another way of grouping the continents is by their north–south position. Continents that lie mainly in the **Northern Hemisphere**—Europe, Asia, and North America—are sometimes grouped together as the northern continents. Continents that lie more in the **Southern Hemisphere**—Africa, South America, Australia, and Antarctica—are sometimes grouped together as the southern continents.

Future changes

Plate tectonics will cause further changes to the continents. In 20 million years, scientists believe that eastern Africa will separate from the rest of the continent along the Great Rift Valley and a sea will be created between these **landmasses.** Some time later, Antarctica will begin to drift slowly to the north. About 180 million years later, the eastern African landmass will collide with Asia, and Antarctica will lie on the **tropical equator!**

The future

We know that the relationships of continents will change over time. Plate **tectonics** will slowly continue to move these great **landmasses** and cause earthquakes and volcanic eruptions. Even with these future dangers, a lot can be done to make the continents safe. Wildlife can be protected from too much hunting and fishing. Land can be protected from **deforestation** and pollution. **Natural resources** can be protected from overuse and waste. And peaceful relations can be promoted between the many different countries and **cultures.**

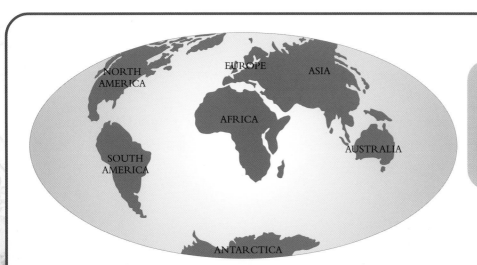

This map shows the possible position of the continents 20 to 50 million years from today.

GLOSSARY

Age of Reptiles time in Earth's history about 250–65 million years ago when reptiles such as dinosaurs were the largest living animals

altitude height of something, especially above sea level

climate kind of weather that occurs in a particular region

colonize settle a region and control the land and its people

conifer non-flowering tree or shrub that has cones and needles

core central part of Earth, made up of solid and molten rock more than 1,865 miles (3,000 kilometers) thick

crust Earth's outermost rock layer

culture ideas, skills, arts, and way of life of a certain people at a certain time. Something that has to do with culture is called cultural.

deciduous tree that sheds its leaves in the fall

deforestation clearing away of trees or forests

delta fan-shaped area formed at the mouth of a river, where the river divides into branches before entering the sea

equator imaginary line around the middle of Earth's surface

exposed laid open to sun, wind, and rain

fertile plain land rich in nutrients and suitable for growing crops and raising livestock

flood plain land made up of soil deposited when a river floods

geographer person who studies Earth's surface

geologist person who studies Earth's rocks and crust

glacier mass of ice that moves slowly across the land

gorge deep, narrow valley with steep walls

gullies narrow channels formed by running water or heavy rains

ice age time when large parts of Earth become colder and are covered by glaciers. There have been many ice ages, but the most recent Ice Age ended over 10,000 years ago.

icebergs masses of floating ice

independent not controlled or supported by others

landmass large area of land, such as a continent

magnetic properties characteristics of a magnet

mantle layer of rock about 1,800 miles (2,900 kilometers) thick that lies below Earth's crust

molten rock rock that has turned to liquid by heat

natural resources supplies of useful materials from nature

Northern Hemisphere northern half of Earth between the North Pole and the equator

Southern Hemisphere southern half of Earth between the South Pole and the equator

tectonic relating to the structure and changes in Earth's crust

temperate moderate; not permanently hot or cold

theory idea, or collection of ideas, put forward to explain certain phenomena or observable events

timber trees or forested land; wood useful for constructing buildings, furniture, and wooden objects

treaties recognized agreements, often between nations, such as an agreement to end war or share resources

tropical of the tropics, the warm regions around the equator

FURTHER READING

Petersen, David. *Africa.* Danbury, Conn.: Children's Press, 1998.

Petersen, David. *Antarctica.* Danbury, Conn.: Children's Press, 1998.

Petersen, David. *Asia.* Danbury, Conn.: Children's Press, 1998.

Petersen, David. *Australia.* Danbury, Conn.: Children's Press, 1998.

Petersen, David. *Europe.* Danbury, Conn.: Children's Press, 1998.

Petersen, David. *North America.* Danbury, Conn.: Children's Press, 1998.

Petersen, David. *South America.* Danbury, Conn.: Children's Press, 1998.

INDEX